Prayers for Writers

a handbook of praying for your writing life

Capital Christian Writers Fellowship

Editors
Stephanie Buckwalter, Johnese Burtram,
Sarah Hamaker, Betsey Kodat

Prayers for Writers
a handbook of praying for your writing life

Copyright ©2020 Capital Christian Writers Fellowship

Stephanie Buckwalter, Johnese Burtram, Sarah Hamaker, Betsey Kodat, Editors
ccwritersfellowship.org

Scripture quotations from the ESV® Bible (The Holy Bible, English Standard Version®), copyright © 2001 by Crossway, a publishing ministry of Good News Publishers. Used by permission. All rights reserved.

Scriptures marked KJV are taken from the KING JAMES VERSION (KJV): KING JAMES VERSION, public domain.

Scripture quotations marked MSG are taken from THE MESSAGE, copyright © 1993, 2002, 2018 by Eugene H. Peterson. Used by permission of NavPress. All rights reserved. Represented by Tyndale House Publishers, a Division of Tyndale House Ministries.

Scriptures marked NASU are taken from the NEW AMERICAN STANDARD UPDATED (NASU): Scripture taken from the NEW AMERICAN STANDARD UPDATED BIBLE®, copyright©, 1995 by The Lockman Foundation. Used by permission.

Scriptures marked NIV are taken from the Holy Bible, New International Version® Copyright © 1973, 1978, 1984, 2011 by Biblica, Inc.® Used by permission. All rights reserved worldwide.

Scripture marked NKJV is taken from the New King James Version®. Copyright © 1982 by Thomas Nelson. Used by permission. All rights reserved.

Cover Design by Samantha Fury

Dedication

To our Father who sent His one and only Son,
Our Lord and Savior Jesus Christ, the Living Word,
who became flesh and lived among us
becoming God with us, and
To the Holy Spirit who breathes life
into our writing.

To Him be honor and glory and praise!
Revelation 5:12

Our Prayer for You

Our heavenly Father, we ask You to raise a chorus of prayer for writing through this book. Favor the writers who use it. Invigorate their prayers and prosper them in their work. Inspire them; give them a way with words; gift them with plots and arguments that reach people. Make their writing worthy of the majestic God that You are. Use their writing to broadcast the beauty of life with You — the hope and health and challenge and wonder of it.

God who hears and answers prayer, unite all who pray using these prayers in the warm fellowship of praying and writing together, as only You can do.

In Jesus' name, Amen.

Stephanie, Johnese, Sarah, and Betsey
CCWF Editorial Team

Table of Contents

Introduction

This book, is for people like you and me — Christians who write. Members of Capital Christian Writers Fellowship (CCWF) submitted prayers for this book to serve as a handbook of encouragement and inspiration for all Christian writers as they fulfill their calling. Christian writers have an amazing mission. We are tasked to express the image of God that we carry as human beings.

Prayer is a huge part of our work. It is "the act of inviting God's presence and power into our [writing]. It is the greatest power available to God's children, and when it is combined with God's word, it is an unstoppable force."[1] Fortunately for us, we have a God who knows writing and a God who invites us to ask Him for help as we write.

As writers, we know we should prioritize prayer. We know that writing is serious business. We know it should be handled with prayer. But sometimes we need to jumpstart and inspire our praying. That is what this book is for — to help stimulate our prayer.

These prayers represent the prayers of a writing community. We called on members to submit prayers. We also held "write-ins," generating prayers together. We sat around a table, thinking.

- We discussed how writers can praise God's character.
- We remembered things writers have to be thankful for.
- We shared the sins and roadblocks that get in the way of our writing.
- We thought about the common needs of writers.
- We planned ways of praying blessings on writers.

Then, scribbling on yellow pads or typing on computers, heads down, hearts open, thoughts flying, we wrote prayers in company with one another. We read our prayers to each other, talked about them, and went back for a second round buoyed up by the synergy of writing together. And we thought about you, our fellow Christian writers. We hope you will find help and comfort and inspiration and strength and vision and hope in these prayers.

Praying in agreement does this incredible thing. It binds us to God and to each other. It helps us realize that, as Jesus promised: *Where two or three are gathered together in my name, there [he is] in the midst of them.* (Matthew 18:20, KJV) Whenever we pray together, Jesus is with us and we become "reckless in our confidence in God, for we begin to realize all the resources of God."[2] Hallelujah!

Stephanie, Johnese, Betsey, Sarah
The CCWF Editorial Team

How to Use This Book

This book is simple to use.

As a tool to help you pray for your writing, it features prayers from our CCWF writers along with a few prayers from other Christian writers throughout Christian history.

Pray prayers from the book in any way you want. Open it at random. Start at the beginning and pray through to the end. Look at the Table of Contents and choose a prayer section.

Write your own prayers. The main purpose of this book is to stimulate your personal prayer. Sections of the book have pages where you can write your own prayers and add scriptures you find to help you in your writing journey.

Share your prayers with others. Email. Letters. In person. When you know fellow writers who are working on a project, send them a written prayer.

Let's raise a chorus of prayers from writers for writers to our great God.

You say grace before meals.
All right.
But I say grace before the play and the opera,
And grace before the concert and pantomime.
And grace before I open a book.
And grace before sketching, painting,
Swimming, fencing, boxing, walking, playing, dancing,
And grace before I dip the pen in ink.[3]

G.K. Chesterton

The prayer preceding all prayers:

"May it be the real me who speaks.
May it be the real Thou that I speak to." [4]

C.S. Lewis

Give yourself to it, [the call to prayer] yield to it; and you
will find not only that you have not been wasting time with
respect to the matter with which you are dealing but that
actually it has helped you greatly in that respect. You will
experience an ease and a facility in understanding what you
were reading, in thinking, in ordering matter for a sermon,
in writing, in everything which is quite astonishing. Such a
call to prayer must never be regarded as a distraction;
always respond to it immediately, and thank God if it
happens to you frequently.[5]

Martyn Lloyd-Jones

Part I
Our Prayers

A Collection

As you read these prayers from other writers, notice the common concerns that we share. Although it is like listening in on a private conversation, it is similar to a conversation any writer might have with God. We learn from listening to each other and echoing scripture as we apply it to our lives.

We hope you enjoy these prayers from your fellow Christian writers. May our prayers become yours.

Dear Lord,

Today I need to write, but quite honestly, I don't feel like it.
I feel discouraged and aware of all my shortcomings.
I know You've given me a writing gift, but I feel inadequate.
I'm tempted to compare myself with others.
Remind me to lean on You, instead of my feelings.

Thank You that writing is hard, because it makes me see my need for You.
Thank You, Lord, that You are the great Creator who creates something out of nothing.
Thank You that You inspire me to write.
Thank You for creative ideas.
Thank You that You help me when I cry out to You.
Thank You, Lord, for the opportunity to write today.
I want to write for Your glory and not my own!
Amen.

Jennifer Hinders

Heavenly Father, Creator God who spoke the world into place and ordered the sun, the moon, and the stars to move in the universe according to Your divine plan—
So order our days.
Bless us with Your presence;
Grant us wisdom and discernment as we settle in to answer Your call to write.
Lord God, as we set aside our plan, our purpose— pour through us Your living water.
Anoint us today with Your Holy Spirit, and let us, as beloved children in Your household, do the work You have given us to do, to lovingly serve You through our writing as faithful witnesses of Your Word.
We thank You, Lord, that this is done in Your Name. Amen and Amen.

Ann Westerman

LORD, You are the Author of my faith; You are the reason I write. My desire to write Your message of salvation, freedom, abundance, and joy comes from You; help me write Your words.

Protect me from compartmentalizing You, LORD. Create in me a driving desire to know You intimately, so I welcome Your infiltration into every area of my life. I'm learning I must submit to Your authority before I can experience the fullness of life You've given to me as a Christ-follower.

Replace my fears with trust in You and Your ways. Teach me to live and write with bold confidence in You. Shield me from the whispering thoughts of my own inadequacies. Remind me it is You in me that will accomplish every good work You planned for me. Lead me, and my readers, to a place of voluntary submission to You, LORD.

Holy Spirit, as I obey, infuse my words with Your power so truth will be evident and offer life to every reader. May what I write reveal You, LORD, and inspire the reader to love You with all their heart, soul, mind, and strength.

May the words come together in such a way as to encourage fearless obedience and promote genuine love for others. May the words I write enable each individual reader to understand their value is based solely on whom You say they are, not what others say of them or even what they think of themselves.

I love writing, LORD. I love the challenge of finding the words to adequately express my thoughts, feelings, and stories.

Thank You for calling me to write. I willingly and intentionally surrender my will, my plan, and my pen to Your will, Your plan, and Your words.
Amen.

Barbara Coulson

Oh, Lord,

You are great indeed. Please come into my mind and encourage my spirit to write — inspire me.

Please guide my mind, my heart, my thinking, and even my fingers as I write Your message. Use me to deliver messages You want to convey in every word, dialogue, theme, setting, character, and plot of my book, whether fiction or creative nonfiction.

Lord, may my writing encourage families and touch the lives of those who are feeling hopeless. Please bring them hope.

Lord, in a world where there is immigration, poverty, alcoholism, infidelity, and suffering, there is also faith, family, love, and strength to overcome life's deep struggles of this earthly existence. Lord, bring blessing to all who read my writing. May it encourage them to persevere in all life's circumstances. May they know that with faith in God all things are possible.

Lord Jesus, Father, Holy Spirit, come and be present with me. Use me to touch the lives of my readers. In Jesus' name, Amen!

Ruth West

Heavenly Father,
You have settled me in this place to write.
    I thank You for this opportunity to put pen to paper —
        fingers to keyboard —
        to write the words You give.

I reject the calling of my "to do" list, the enticing lure of
      books half-read, of computer games or Facebook,
      email or calls to friends.
I set these aside with every sense of fear, or feelings of
      despair, or lack of talent.

Heavenly Father,
You have shown me the steps and shined Your light on the
path ahead. You have impacted my dreams and given me
visions of stories.
      I would write the visions You give.
      I would listen to know the characters walking through
            my head and step away to give them the freedom
            to speak Your Word as they will.
      Stir the hearts of any who read to give You glory.
         In Jesus' name, Amen.

Ann Westerman

Dear Jesus,

Please guide my writing today. Help me to write for an
audience of One, striving to please You first and man
second. Give me the right words to bring glory to You.

Keep my heart attuned to the things of heaven, rather than
the things of earth. Don't let my desire for earthly success
draw my attention away from my Savior. Give me a humble
and teachable spirit, never thinking I am above learning or
too busy to lend a hand to a fellow writer.

When I find myself discouraged, let me find comfort in Your scriptures. When I find myself wanting more than You've seen fit to give me, let me rest in the knowledge that I am exactly where I need to be on my writing journey.

Help me not lose heart when the days are dark. Help me to seek after You when my heart hurts from rejection. Let me see glimpses of how my life is furthering Your kingdom.

Above all, allow my words to bring the light of Christ to those who read them. May my love for You shine through all that I write, even when I don't mention Your precious name.

May I write for Your glory and may You use my writing for my own good.

Amen.

Sarah Hamaker

Father in Heaven,

As You give to me themes, plots, conflicts, and characters who live and breathe on the pages I write, I thank You for the readers You will draw to these stories and right now lift them up to You for Your blessing.

In Jesus' name, Amen.

Ann Westerman

Lord,

You are the Author of language.
You are the Word of Life.
You are the Author and Perfecter of our faith.

May Your words flow through the hands of those of us You
    have called to write.
May we speak Truth, Your Truth, in everything, always
    mindful that we are in a battle with an evil being whose
    only real weapon is deceit.
May the Truth in our writing draw our readers to You.
May we, Your writers, let our lights so shine before men that
    they may see the Truth and glorify You in heaven.
May the words of our pens and every meditation of our
    hearts by pleasing to You, O Lord, our Rock and our
    Redeemer, as we write for Your glory. Amen.
(References: Hebrews 12:2, NASB; 1John 1:1, NIV; Revelation 12:9, ESV;
Matthew 5:16, NASB; Psalm 19:4, NIV)

Stephanie Buckwalter

Father God,

You are the Author and Perfecter of our faith (Hebrews 12:2,
NASB) and I pray that You will help me as I author words
that will bring You honor and glory, and breathe hope and
grace into the hearts of my readers.

Help me not to get distracted by busyness, but to be focused
on the calling You have given me as a writer.

Help me not to get paralyzed by doubt or fear, but to write
with courage and confidence and obedience in my calling.

Help me to focus on my readers, on their needs and struggles and desires; to write with a sense of urgency and purpose the words they need to hear from You; words burning in my heart to share with them.

Help me to get out of the way, to let Your words flow through my pen.

Holy Spirit, You are welcome here. Strengthen and guide every word I write. Help align my motivations and desires with Yours. Amen.

Jenn Soehnlin

Oh, Lord, without You in the midst
　　as the Author of —
　　　　the Annointer of —
　　　　the Inspirer of our stories,
　　as the Wisdom Giver —
　　　　the Empowerer —
　　　　　　our plans fall into ruin and confusion.
Let us always lean on You,
　　　　rely on You,
　　　　listen to You,
　　　　　　for Your inspiration
As we settle in to write today the story You have put
　　in our hearts to write.
　　　　In Jesus' name, Amen.

Ann Westerman

Sometimes, Father, my writing carries me away with ease and wonder into a land of intense expression where I am completely lost in my work. Sometimes I seem to get it just right and it flows from me with joy.

Other times, I'm drier than the Mojave Desert. Getting an idea out of me is like calling for water from a stone. Finding an idea or crafting one sentence is like a marathon. I seem to be the dullest, slowest, least fluent person on earth.

Most times, it is just ordinary me, typing away and putting ideas down, looking over the words, consulting the thesaurus, tweaking the phrases. Pondering, changing my tack, tearing it up. Rereading the whole.

And almost always, the process shocks me into knowing how much I need You. When it is easy, I need You. When it is impossible, I need You. When it is ordinary work, I need You. But isn't that just what You do—help the needy? You are the God of miracles who brings water from a stone and blooms in the desert.

So I ask You: Be my inspiration, my editor, my publisher, my friend-in-writing, my audience. I want to write in the circle of Your influence—pour Your favor on me.

You know, God, that I need flesh and blood friends, readers, editors, and publishers. You know that I need perseverance and a work ethic and time, and I trust You for them all. I trust You for everything.

In Jesus' name, Amen.

Betsey Kodat

Lord,

I come to Your presence in awe — of everything You are — and all You have made me to be. I'm humbled by Your omniscience and Your ever-faithful promise to use my gifts for Your glory.

I pray for guidance as I attempt to shine Your light in this world. Whether it's through the flicker of a well-chosen word or the flame of a life-changing story, I ask that Your name shine brighter than a thousand suns.

I ask for clarity, that You will reveal the words You would have me write. Please keep my focus on You, and never on things of this world. Help me never view writing as simply a job, but as an avenue through which I fulfill Your purpose.

Bless the LORD, *O my soul; And all that is within me,* bless *His holy name!* (Psalm 103:1, KJV)

For I know the thoughts that I think toward you, saith the LORD, *thoughts of peace, and not of evil, to give you an expected end.* (Jeremiah 29:11, KJV)

Audra Sanlyn

Heavenly Father,

I surrender my writing, my words, my message, my platform-building efforts to You. I do not want to be writing and building without You, for it is toiling in vain.

Help me to keep You in the center of all my motivations and my writing. Without You in it, it is void of purpose and joy and Your blessing.

You are the Word and You gave me words to say that will breathe Your hope, joy, peace, and grace into our lives. May I be Your mouthpiece that speaks to the hearts of readers with the words You long for them to hear.

Help me to get out of the way, to let go of my distractions and doubts and fears to focus on You and Your will for my writing.

Help me to use the gifts and talents and passions You have given me as a writer. Help me to not bury it, as one of the servants did (Matthew 25:15-30), but to invest in it, to nurture and grow and steward and use my gifts of writing. Help me to share those gifts boldly, without fear.

Help my motivations in writing to be to bring You glory and to be obedient to share the giftings and the messages You have given me.

May I strive for Your approval in my writing, and not the approval of others. (Galatians 1:10)

Use my writing for Your honor and glory. Amen.

Jenn Soehnlin

A Prayer for the Misbegotten

And Jesus said to them, "I am the bread of life. He who comes to Me shall never hunger, and he who believes in Me shall never thirst." (John 6:35, NKJV)

Heavenly Father, I know You are good. At Your core, You are the best God that anyone could imagine. You saved me by the sacrifice of Your only Son, Jesus. Your word says that Jesus is the bread of life. After coming to him, I would never hunger or thirst again. On a deep, spiritual level, I know that word is true. In my mind and emotions, I find myself hungering for personal success.

Sometimes, the adoration of readers feels like the most delicious cold drink on a hot day. Like a misbegotten lost soul, occasionally my heart longs for earthly fame, riches to spend on my wants, and praise to feed my ego.

Teach me instead to be satisfied with Your approval. When I write, guide me each step of the way. Allow me to lose myself in Your Spirit so that His words speak, instead of my own. Fill me with Your message for today. When I've eaten of the manna You provide, let me rise from my keyboard full and complete in my relationship with You. May I hunger no more for anything but Your presence.

In the name of Jesus I pray, Amen.

David Winters

God's Word Today

We are God's hands and heart and words here on this earth, just like the saints were of old; Jesus called them and us to do *even greater works* than He did. (John 14:12, NLT)

So when I question, "Who am I am to write modern-day Bible stories? Who do I think I am to take an Old Testament story and re-imagine it for today's world with modern characters, settings, and plots?"

I think of some of the Old Testament writers…
    Moses, David, Solomon, Isaiah;
and the Gospel writers…
    Matthew, Mark, Luke, and John.

They were probably like me when God called them, too.
And without what they wrote there would be
    no Bible,
    no Good News.
What they wrote was radical for their time. What I write may be considered edgy…but so I am called. And I need to write it so that Christians today get the message God wants them to hear.

So I put
    my ego,
    my shortcomings,
    my false pride
aside and say
    get behind me Satan. (Matt 16:23, NIV)
I have God's work to do and only I can do it.

He must have called me for a reason.
He has called you, too…

And only you can write the words He has inscribed on your soul. Only you can be His hands and heart here on this earth.

We are on a mission, unique yet united,
    and if we don't go forth, His message will be lost.

Sometimes it is hard, and like any mission, there will be
    doubters and naysayers,
    challenges and roadblocks.
But just like we pick up our crosses,
I pray we all pick up our pens and use them
    reverently,
    thoughtfully,
    prayerfully
to do His will and spread His Word —
    to have the courage of the saints to answer His call.

Michele Chynoweth

A Prayer for the Lonely Author

Dear Lord,

I'm lonely. It's a weekday, and those I love are off working at their jobs. Some are in bright and beautiful offices that buzz with activity. Others are laughing with a work friend or standing in line to buy coffee at the convenience store. The kids are at school. Watch over them.

You and I are sitting here at my computer. It seems like a year ago that I went to that writer's conference. Has it just been a week? The many hugs and words of friendly encouragement nourished my soul. The excitement of the new authors fueled my desire to get another book out yesterday. My notes remind me of the new skills I learned. Thank You for the fuel You give me to start writing again today.

Thank You for being my companion as I write. Praise Your name for faithfully guiding my mind and fingers. Help me to write Your answers for a world that needs You so badly. Let's get going! Amen.

David Winters

Thank You, Lord, for the gift of words!

From the beginning of time, You worked through the creative and spoken word. This is so intrinsic to You that John called You the Word. What a joy that You bring us alongside You as we express ourselves in the words that You give us!

Oh, that my words were recorded, that they were written on a scroll, that they were inscribed with an iron tool on lead or engraved in rock forever! (Job 19:23-24, NIV)

Sometimes, though, the words don't come easily. What is a writer who cannot write? What do I do when the longing in my heart to compose prayers to honor You does not bear fruit?

Father God, center me in You. Remind me that in You, there is no such thing as writer's block. While I feel impeded, I feel that my creativity is cut off, You do not operate by feelings. The heavenly realm, all under Your control, operates by faith. *For we live by faith, not by sight.* (2 Corinthians 5:7, NIV) In faith, guide the words that I write today.

Excellent and godly writing often takes more work than we think it should. We know what we want to convey or what we think our message should be. However, we are finite beings trying to touch the infinite. Only the Spirit within us can understand what needs to be said. Only He can guide our craft and practice of writing. *May these words of my mouth and this meditation of my heart, be pleasing in your sight, LORD, my Rock and my Redeemer.* (Psalm 19:14, NIV)

Lord, my writing is in Your hands and Your times. Guide my pen and my keyboard to say the words You want said. And when they don't come easily, remind me that even a word in Your honor is a step forward. Help me to step into Your will and glorify You, one word at a time. Whether the words come easily or not, God, I am Your writer. Do with me what You will.

My friends and fellow writers also encounter struggles. Be with each one as he or she strives to serve You. Affirm that my writing friends are still writers on days they cannot write. Call them anew and give them strength, Lord!

Susan Lyttek

The Storyteller's Prayer

Holy Father,

For Your willingness to condescend to our level of understanding, we offer praise and glory to Your name, great author of our faith. (Hebrews 12:2, KJV)

Forgive us, Lord, for putting on airs and speaking above the comprehension of our readers and listeners, thinking that we are better than they are.

Yet we give thanks for the gifts and talents that You have given us in the written and spoken word.

In the power of Your Holy Spirit, lead us down the storylines that You would have us tell. Help us to show only what You would have us write.

May our writing always lift up our readers and point them to You.

In Jesus' precious name, Amen.

Stephen Hiemstra

Dear Lord,

We want our writing and our words to bless those who read what we write.

Please help us to be motivated in our hearts to write, not for wealth or reputation or to please ourselves, but to be a blessing to others, to Your glory.

Please give us a heart for our brothers and sisters; for all people. Help us to remember that every person is made in Your image and that You love every single person. You died for every person who will pick up our book or read our article or listen to our writing in audio form. You know them, and You care about them. Please empower us to know and care about them as well.

We ask You to give us hearts that love. We hold on to Your promise, *A new heart also will I give you, and a new spirit will I put within you.* (Ezekiel 36:26, KJV) You have also promised that Your *love has been poured out into our hearts through the Holy Spirit.* (Romans 5:5, NIV) We want to overflow with Your love to others.

Please grant us knowledge of our readers' deepest needs and fears and desires, so we might minister to them through Your power, Your Spirit.

Please mold and shape and form our writing that it might *encourage one another and build one another up.*
(1 Thessalonians 5:11, ESV); and that we may *give grace to those who hear.* (Ephesians 4:29, ESV)

Please help our writing to motivate and inspire others, letting us consider *"how to stir up one another to love and good works."* (Hebrews 10:24, ESV)

We ask You for wisdom, insight, and discernment always to write what is Your best purpose for others. We remember that *Like cold water to a weary soul is good news from a distant land.* (Proverbs 25:25, NIV) We have the good news of the gospel to share with others in a way that they can hear.

We pray in the name of Jesus, Amen.

Joe Gelak

Rejoice in the Success of Others

Rejoice in the Lord always; again I will say, rejoice.
Philippians 4:4 (ESV)

Dear Lord God,

I am a frail human, one prone to suffer from envy and jealousy, especially in relation to my writing. I often take my eyes off my own journey and long for the greener pastures of my fellow writers.

Help me, Lord, to tamp down the ugly beast of jealousy and to raise up in my heart a thankfulness for the success of others. May I replace envy with rejoicing and truly come to have a heart that cheerleads for others and their writing success.

Let me be among the first to congratulate writers I know personally with sincere words of praise and affirmation. Let my heart long to have opportunities to celebrate the success of other writers.

Root out my own ambition that would tell me that another's success detracts from my own. Tear out my own tendency to smile on the outside but grumble on the inside when others succeed where I am not or when others receive more accolades or sales than my own work.

Let me see the truth that to rejoice in the good work God is doing in other Christian writers is an integral part of my own writing life. Give me opportunities to put this into practice, and let my words be an encouragement to those writers.

Above all, let me rejoice in the success of others because in doing so, I am pleasing You, my Heavenly Father, and author and finisher of my faith. Amen.

Sarah Hamaker

Part II
The Reason You Write

Consider the Reason You Write

Every writer has a reason for writing, a cherished desire or a dream about what he or she wants to accomplish. What is your reason for writing? You may want to write for a living and respond to market needs, or you may just want to write for fun, like a travelogue or a book for your children or a family memoir.

Whatever your reason for writing, we encourage you, as a Christian writer, to clarify your purpose by writing it down. Somehow thinking becomes clearer when it is written down.

Take time to consider the spiritual dimension of your writing. What part do you believe God plays in the purpose for your writing? Ask the Holy Spirit to speak to you as you explore your purpose.

By and large a good rule for finding out is this: the kind of work God usually calls you to is the kind of work a) that you need most to do and b) the world most needs to have done. If you really get a kick out of your work, you've presumably met requirement a), but if your work is writing TV deodorant commercials, the chances are you've missed requirement b).[6]

Frederick Buechner

The Lord's Prayer

The Lord's Prayer is like God's mission statement, and God invites us to pray it with Him. When we pray a variation like this, we remind ourselves that our writing mission is part of the larger mission of God.

Our Father, who art in heaven,
May I write to honor and broadcast Your character to the world.
Inspire and guide my writing so that others may know the truth of Your kingdom and be set free.
Inspire and guide my writing so that the world may learn what it means to do Your will here on earth.
Nourish my soul and sustain my writing to represent You well.
Forgive me whenever I write selfishly or fail to tell the truth about life.
May I be gracious and forgiving towards all I meet in the writing world.
Save me from evil and may my writing be full of goodness.
For Thine is the kingdom and the power and the glory for ever and ever. Amen.

Betsey Kodat

Articulate the Reason You Write

May God help you clarify your mission so that you know what you are to write and why. May you wait on Him as you articulate the reason you write.

What do you want to write? What do you feel uniquely gifted (or called) to write?

What do you want your writing to accomplish? What values do you want your writing to communicate?

How can you reflect biblical values in your writing?

Who are you writing for?

Write Your Mission Statement

As you ponder what your heart desires to write, formulate your thoughts into a mission statement of one or two sentences. A mission statement gives you a tool to remember what you want to write and why. It keeps you focused, helps you make your goals, and stay in touch with God so you can be true to the personal writing mission God has entrusted to you.

Example
I want to leave a legacy of written prayer for my daughters so they may be moved to pray and experience Your love through prayer.

Write your mission statement

Turn your mission statement into a prayer

Examples

Father, show me how to leave a legacy of prayer for my daughters so they will also learn to pray and maximize prayer in their lives.

Father, help me collect my memories into a coherent whole so they will be enjoyable to read. Help me find the right people to read my work and comment on it.

Father, "always call me back to your best plans." [7]

Kevin Johnson

Lord,
You have called me to write.
Your message is my message. My story is Your story, expressed through my life. I ask for words to express the love You have for Your creation.

May that love, that desire for relationship, cry out to those who are hurting, to those with ears to hear. Amen.

Stephanie Buckwalter

As one called to write Your message, let me use the passions You have placed in my heart to guide my writing.

Lord, let me accurately mirror Your heart for this earth and the people of this world. I want my writing to reflect Your divine nature, not merely my own sentiments. May Your message of redemption and reconciliation permeate all my writing. Please help me to write with honesty, clarity, and compassion.

Keep me focused on Your mission, to seek and save the lost. (Luke 19:10)

In the name of Jesus.

Johnese Burtram

--------♦◊♦◊♦◊♦--------

Write your mission statement as a prayer

Part III
Your Prayers

Prayers for Preparation to Write

Praise and Thanksgiving

Before you write, make your first act of composing praising and thanking God. By doing this, you orient yourself and your writing to the proper context. Writers tend to think of the complexities or problems or situations they face. But when you magnify God, remembering what He has done, you begin to write in a context of faith.

Praise God for who He is—the greatest, most creative Author of all. All-powerful. Omni-benevolent. Ever-present. Eternal. Grace-filled. Forgiving. Wise. The one who knows you and your readers and your publishers and everyone involved in your writing life. The Sovereign Orchestrator of everything that happens.

Thank Him for what He has given you and done for you. Education. Homes. Meals. Past writing. Unexpected providences. Ideas. Happiness, sadness, and everything in between. The place you live. Family. The Bible. Friends. Computers. Publishers. Editors. Writing groups. All the books in the world.

God has given us so much. May He give us one more thing: A heart to praise and thank Him.

Praise God from whom all blessings flow.

You are worthy to be praised!

We sing glory and honor and praise to You, O Lord.

Litany of Writer's Praise

I praise You, Father, for who You are. As a writer, I delight in Your multidimensional character and what You mean to me.

I praise You that You were the first communicator. You told creation to stand up and it did. By a word You created the universe in all its beauty and diversity. You sent Your Son, the Word of God.

I praise You, Lord God, that You are the all-present God, present with me. You are both audience to what I write and inspiration to what I write.

Lord, I praise You that You are the inspiration behind all words, all thoughts, all books, all communication.

Betsey Kodat

The LORD is my strength and my defense;
he has become my salvation.
He is my God, and I will praise him, my
father's God, and I will exalt him.
Exodus 15:2 (NIV)

We must, during all our labour and in all else we do, even in our reading and writing, holy though both may be – I say more, even during our formal devotions and spoken prayers – pause for some short moment, as often indeed as we can, to worship God in the depth of our heart, to savour Him, though it be but in passing, and as it were by stealth. Since you are not unaware that God is present before you whatever you are doing, that He is at the depth and centre of your soul, why not then pause from time to time at least from that which occupies you outwardly, even from your spoken prayers, to worship Him inwardly, to praise Him, petition Him, to offer Him your heart and thank Him? What can God have that gives Him greater satisfaction than that a thousand times a day all His creatures should thus pause to withdraw and worship him in the heart?[8]

Brother Lawrence

I will praise the LORD, who counsels me;
even at night my heart instructs me.
Psalm 16:7 (NIV)

Thank You, God, for my little flask of oil –
A nub of pencil, the back of an envelope, a moment
    of quiet –
That I use to describe the room, start the conversation,
    tighten the action.
A few inches of text, new or better, are enough for today,
And more than enough to give me hope for oil in my flask
    tomorrow.[9]

Elizabeth Vander Lei

Holy, holy, holy art Thou, Lord God.
You, Creator God of all,
You, Setter of sun and moon and stars in their place,
You, Winder-up of the universe with all its
moving parts
of seasons, of wind and tides.

With hearts on fire with awe and love for You,
We praise You,
We magnify You.
You, the Alpha and Omega, Lord of Lords, King of
Kings.
Holy, holy, holy art Thou, Lord God.

Ann Westerman

Give thanks to the LORD, for he is good;
his love endures forever.
1 Chronicles 16:34 (NIV)

Lord, You weave our lives together as a great tapestry, a continuous story throughout the ages. The threads of our lives intersect and run alongside one another, influencing the design. We humbly recognize that our writing is part of that tapestry. As we share our tragedies and triumphs, our struggles and soaring victories, we recognize themes common to the human condition, with variations in each of our lives. Each theme, each variation, is an opportunity to spur others on to praise and thanksgiving—regardless of circumstances. Because You are the weaver of the story, we recognize that *From you comes the theme of [our] praise in the great assembly.* (Psalm 22:25, NIV) May we be found faithful.

Stephanie Buckwalter

Praise the LORD. Praise God in his
sanctuary;
praise him in his mighty heavens.
Praise him for his acts of power;
praise him for his surpassing greatness.
Praise him with the sounding of the
trumpet,
praise him with the harp and lyre,
praise him with timbrel and dancing,
praise him with the strings and pipe,
praise him with the clash of cymbals,
praise him with resounding cymbals.
Let everything that has breath praise the
LORD.
Praise the LORD.
Psalm 150 (NIV)

Praise You, God, You are the Living Word, raw communication at its best, not needing translation or effort to understand. Your communication is new every day; You can speak right to the heart.

Jesus, in You are all the treasures I need as a writer, all the treasures of wisdom and knowledge. (Colossians 2:3)

For library stacks,
For the bookstore café
The study carrel,
The ample desk —
    praise.

For the cloud of witnesses ranged on the bookshelves,
For the challenge of an empty page.
For the dream that awakens me,
The faith that persists after the rejection letter,
The hope I slide into a new manila envelope
The joy you give me through this work —
    praise.

For the grand symphony of language,
For the hardware of grammar,
For the infinite palette of words,
The game of it all,
This bounteous feast —
    praise, all praise.[10]

Elizabeth Stickney

I will give thanks to the Lord because of his righteousness; I will sing the praises of the name of the Lord Most High.
Psalm 7:17 (NIV)

Father, thank You for the King James Version of the Bible, the bold translation which has enlivened the English language down to our very day. Thank You that Christians have always been on the forefront of teaching literacy so that all may communicate through reading and writing.

I thank You, Lord, for the gift of writing, as a means of expressing ourselves as Your children. I thank You for fluency and power in communication, and for those who are gifted in this area.

I thank You, Father, for the many hours I've spent enjoying books, thinking and learning and pondering what someone said.

Father, I thank You that You are the God of story. You write events that lead to a conclusion; You work through us. We get to be part of Your story.

I thank You, Lord, for all forms of media and social media, for libraries, books, publishers, newspapers, and journalists.

Betsey Kodat

I will extol the LORD at all times;
his praise will always be on my lips.
Psalm 34:1 (NIV)

We thank you for writers who wake us up,
Who call us to attention;
We thank you for authors who craft words
That reverberate in our ears and in our hearts.[11]

Susan Felch

Litany of Thanksgiving

Let us give thanks to God our Father for all his gifts so freely bestowed upon us.

For the beauty and wonder of your creation in earth and sky and sea,
We thank you, Lord.

For all that is gracious in the lives of men and women, revealing the image of Christ,
We thank you, Lord. …

For minds to think, and hearts to love, and hands to serve,
We thank you, Lord.

For health and strength to work, and leisure to rest and play,
We thank you, Lord. …

For all valiant seekers after truth, liberty, and justice,
We thank you, Lord. …

Above all, we give you thanks for the great mercies and promises given to us in Christ Jesus our Lord;

To him be praise and glory, with you,
O Father, and the Holy Spirit, now and forever.
Amen.[12]

Book of Common Prayer

Stand up and praise the LORD your God,
who is from everlasting to everlasting.
Blessed be your glorious name, and may
it be exalted above all blessing and
praise. You alone are the LORD. You made
the heavens, even the highest heavens,
and all their starry host, the earth and all
that is on it, the seas and all that is in
them. You give life to everything, and the
multitudes of heaven worship you.
Nehemiah 9:5-6 (NIV)

I will thank God for the pleasures given me through my senses, for the glory of the thunder, for the mystery of music, the singing of birds and the laughter of children. I will thank God for the pleasures of seeing, …Truly, oh, Lord, the earth is full of Thy riches! And yet, how much more I will thank and praise God for the strength of my body enabling me to work, …for the gift of my mind, …for his loving guidance of my mind ever since it first began to think, and of my heart ever since it first began to love.[13]

Edward King

Enter his gates with thanksgiving and his
courts with praise; give thanks to him
and praise his name
Psalm 100:4 (NIV)

Writing your own prayers of praise and thanksgiving

May God help you to worship and thank Him for who He is and what He does for you as a writer.

Related to God's character, what influences your writing? What aspect of His character do you especially need? (Presence? Wisdom? Kindness? Availability? Guiding?)

What are you thankful for?

Think of your problems and roadblocks to writing as reasons for praise and thanksgiving. (Antagonism? Doldrums in writing? A rejection? Lost zeal?) God responds powerfully to praise. Without minimizing your problems, magnify God in spite of them. (1 Thessalonians 5:18)

Write your prayers of praise and thanksgiving

Silence, Solitude, and Surrender

In a world filled with chaos and noise, we need to learn the disciplines of silence and solitude. Scripture is replete with the admonition to wait on the Lord and be silent in His presence. The story of Elijah in 1 Kings 19 finds the prophet hiding in the cave of Horeb where he experiences cataclysmic demonstrations of God's power, only to discover the voice of God is not in *a great and powerful wind* that *tore the mountains apart and shattered the rocks* but after the wind, the earthquake and the fire, in *a gentle whisper.* (1 Kings 19:11-12, NIV)

When the chaos and noise of your life is silenced, then in the stillness, as you wait on the Lord, in surrender to His will, can you hear His word in your spirit. When you have heard His word, you can write with confidence that you are writing what God wants you to write.

Father,

Give me the strength of silence in Your presence. There is so much going on around me—a tsunami of activity inside my thoughts and outside in my everyday life. Have mercy on me and teach me the truth that in quiet and trust is my strength.

In Jesus' name, Amen.

This is what the Sovereign LORD, the Holy One of Israel, says: In repentance and rest is your salvation, in quietness and trust is your strength. (Isaiah 30:15, NIV)

Betsey Kodat

Writers God-Inspired

Our matchless, compassionate, merciful God, and Creator, May Your Word be a lamp to my feet and a light to my path. (Psalm 119:105, ESV). All life, the heavens, earth, and seas began at Your Word. Your Word creates beauty, wholeness, and wonder.

As You called life and order from chaos, please guide our thoughts, imaginings, creativity, and hearts to write in such a way that mountains are moved and thrown into the sea. God, make us vessels of honor. Order our steps, direct our choices, and enlighten our thinking that our offering will be pleasing and acceptable in Your sight.

Help us so that we —
 Will be still and know You, God! (Psalm 46:10)
 See with Your eyes and listen for Your voice.
 Craft language and works of art from life experiences,
  engaging our mind, body, soul, and spirit to please
  You and influence our readers.
 Embrace life's lessons birthed in deep pains and
  healings, losses and victories, sadness and joy, losses
  and gains, fatigue and rest, disaster and recovery,
  failure and achievement, deficits and windfalls,
  deserts and waterfalls, valleys and mountaintops.

And, above all things, help us so that we —
 Daily enter Your Presence,
 Inspire audiences through God-anointed words,
  imagery, and emotions.
 And, glorify You through our lives and writing.
In Jesus' name we pray, Amen.

Sharon Holmes

Thou takest the pen—and the lines dance.
Thou takest the flute—and the notes shimmer.
Thou takest the brush—and the colors sing.
So all things have meaning and beauty in that space beyond
time where Thou art. How then can I hold back anything
from Thee?[14]

Dag Hammarskjold

God be in my head and in my understanding;
God be in my eyes, and in my looking;
God be in my mouth, and in my speaking;
God be in my heart, and in my thinking;
God be at my end, and at my departing. [15]

Sarum Primer, 1538

*Be still before the LORD and wait patiently
for Him.*
Psalm 37:7 (NIV)

Lord Jesus,

You know all the words and ideas that swirl about in my
head.
Are these Your words, or just figments of my own
imaginations?
Still the cacophony of this world.
Quiet me in Your presence as I wait on You.
I want the voice enlivening my words to be Yours and not
my own. Amen.

Johnese Burtram

Writing your own prayers of silence and submission

May God help you to still yourself before Him, to begin with Him, to put yourself into His hands, and to submit yourself to Him.

What things trouble you? What do you need to turn over to God?

How can you offer yourself to God as a writer?

Write your prayers for silence and submission

Confession

There are sins which are especially tempting to writers (i.e., making an idol of writing, over-concentrating on writing and neglecting other responsibilities, not working on your craft, expecting God miraculously to make you write well, failing to trust God). Sin is a roadblock in your writing path — it is a cancer that will nullify your best writing. Confessing frees you and clears the path to your best writing. When you confess, you can sit down before your computer fresh and ready to write.

Father God, you are the Author of stories great and small. Forgive me for sometimes thinking that inspiration comes only from the great stories, the powerful narratives, the lyric instances of profound beauty breaking forth on our senses. …Help me to listen to the ordinary things people tell me. Make me attend to how they speak and to the yearnings of their hearts that emerge in such daily conversation.[16]

Scott Hoezee

As the beauty of creation calls to men's hearts,
may my writing draw men to the Creator.
    Clear my mind of all distractions,
    of the worries of this life.
    Guard me from promoting worldly ideas
    that set other things above You.
You alone are worthy to be praised.
May You be high and lifted up in all that I write today.
Amen.

Stephanie Buckwalter

An Untarnished Heart

Father,

Forgive me for overestimating or underestimating
my power as a writer.

Give me humility and a teachable spirit.

My dreams are good,
but forgive me when they become an idol
that is more important to me than You or my loved ones are.

Forgive me for selfishness,
 a sin which will tarnish my writing.

Betsey Kodat

As I prepare to write, help me, Lord, to listen to You. Grant
me the stillness of soul needed to sense Your presence. Help
me to turn away from the chaos of life and wait in silence to
discern what You are saying to me that needs to be shared
with others.

Help me Lord, to relinquish my fear and my pride. Help me
to get a true view of who You are and who I am.

I surrender my fear of rejection to You. I make You my
audience of One.

Be pleased, my God, with the words of my mouth, the
meditation of my heart, and the message of my pen.

Johnese Burtram

For the times I've made my writing my idol —
     Good Lord, forgive me. ...

For my vexations when people would not bow down and
       worship my idol—
    by interrupting me when I am writing,
    by valuing my writing less than I do,
    by becoming upset when my writing takes precedence
     over our common and necessary labors...
    Good Lord, forgive me.

For the times when I have forgotten to thank you for
     having granted me the ability to write,
    or to praise you for the vocation —
    Good Lord, forgive me. ...

Because you do forgive me, and because you are my God
     forever,
    I praise you, good Lord.[17]

Walter Wangerin, Jr.

Father, don't let me sin by procrastination and not doing the
work You have given me to do.

Writing your own prayers of confession

May God open your eyes to any hidden sin in you. May He be so kind as to inspire you to confess so you can receive His lavish, generous forgiveness.

What sin or wrongdoing do you need to admit to God? Be open and vulnerable. Don't defend yourself — be fearless in searching for any wrongdoing so it can be dealt with.

Write your prayers of confession

Prayers for Yourself as a Writer

Your uniqueness is critical to the whole endeavor of writing. Every author is individual and that is what makes each piece of writing one-of-a-kind. In writing Scripture, God used the writer's individual personality, knowledge, background, vocabulary, and style to shine through every verse they wrote. The Holy Spirit gave them wisdom and insight, but they made their own choices about content, form, and style just as you or I do whenever we write. [18] While you don't write Scripture, the same Holy Spirit can inspire you. You are the main tool of your own craft—God will use *you* to write.

Come, Lord Jesus, help me to fight through any frustration and be an overcomer. I can do all things through You who give me hope and strength for each day and writing period.

Help me to write life-changing words for my readers so they come to know God, the Lord Jesus, as their Savior.

Ruth West

Oh, place my words in the kiln of your heart that
    they may be enduring and strong,
    tempered and seasoned with love and resilience.
Give me a well-trained tongue
    that has been borne out of silent listening in the
    sanctuary of my heart.
May my words become love in the lives of others.[19]

Macrina Wiederkehr

Lord,

I have committed myself to write regularly — not just when the notion strikes me, but as a discipline.

Help me to put my fears aside, boot up the computer, and just start.

Give me focus and clarity of thought. Let my ideas fall into place, organized and clear.

I am answering Your call to write. Help me not to be distracted by the urgent but discern the important.

Grant that I will be carried along by Your Spirit as I devote this writing task to You. Amen.

Johnese Burtram

Father, show me "what it means to live out a calling to write in this world of beauty, grace and order — and ugliness, hatred, and chaos."[20]

Gary Schmidt

Lord, to the end that my heart may think, that my pen may write, and that my mouth may set forth Thy praise, pour forth into my heart and pen and mouth Thy grace.[21]

Bernard of Cluny

Heavenly Father,

I am grateful for the opportunity to be a writer and to share my words and ideas with others. I thank Thee for allowing me the opportunity to be, in small part, as Thou art: a creator. I'm grateful too for the blessings that flow from editors, publishers, and of course, from readers. As I begin this new project, I am filled with self-doubt, second thoughts, and outright fear. Please give me the strength to take this leap of faith and the courage to face the blank page. Grant me the faith — no, the sure knowledge — that if I will put my trust in Thee and write even one sentence, a second will surely follow.[22]

Chris Crowe

Make me into Your writer, Lord. Sharpen my gifts, keep me humble, polish my sense of humor, and make my mind alert to all that You do.

Father, help me to be faithful to care for the gifts You have given me. Let me shape them and hone them and use them for Your glory.

May every part of my writing be fully human so that You can fill it with Your greatness and power and glory and beauty.

Father, writing is a journey I want to make with You. Please don't let me go alone.

Betsey Kodat

Holy Father, Almighty and ever-living God,

Holy, holy, holy, art Thou and worthy of all glory, all honor, all praise.

Teach me, Lord, to number my days and strengthen me to finish this race You have set before me.

Help me, Lord, to set aside fear, to set aside procrastination, and to do all as for You and not for men.

Grant me Your wisdom and discernment to finish each story, each poem, and/or each essay You call me to write, and then, in obedience to Your call, to write the next.

Anoint the words I write so that through them will flow Your living Word to touch each reader's heart and mind and soul that they will turn to You and give You the glory.

Into Your hands, I place this day and this work.

In Jesus' name, Amen.

Ann Westerman

Father, let me incarnate my idea, embodiment of the sentiment, the manifestation of the concept, the enfleshing of the meaning. It is to make physical, the abstract. To bring into the world what was not in this form brought into the world before.[23]

Betsey Kodat

Lord, bless this writer as she seeks to communicate with clarity and precision the message You have given her.

Make her courageous and brave when she shares the challenging message.

Make her gentle and compassionate as she shares Your caring heart.

Make her humble as she sees the good fruit born out of her obedience to Your call.

Bless her with Your shalom.

Johnese Burtram

The lips of the righteous nourish many.
Proverbs 10:21 (NIV)

Lord,

I run into so many roadblocks to writing.
Most of them are of my own making:
fearing my vision is too narrow;
that my words will be unskilled in capturing it;
that I do not know enough.
It's the whole idea — who am I to write this?

Betsey Kodat

Facing a Hostile Response

Take Thee again another roll, and write in it all the former words there were in the first roll, which Jehoiakim, the king of Judah hath burned. (Jeremiah 36:28, KJV)

Father,

We bless Your name and give You all praise, because You alone are worthy of praise, honor, and glory.

We ask, in the name of our Lord and Savior, Jesus Christ, that You grant us courage to write the words that You have instructed us to write. Strengthen us, as we write in a world that desperately needs You, in opposition of the enemy who is determined to destroy the message and the messenger.

Thank You for Your Holy Spirit, who intercedes for us in groans beyond our words. In the name of our Lord Jesus Christ, we make our petition. Amen.

Sharron Giambanco

Lord,

Thank You that I am fearfully and wonderfully made. There is no one else in all of creation with my fingerprints, my background, my thoughts, or my way of presenting ideas. I am truly unique in all of creation, and You call me by name. I celebrate my uniqueness and refuse to compare myself to other writers or other people's ministry of words. You have created works for me to walk in. I embrace those works. Amen.

Stephanie Buckwalter

Lord,

Writing is one of the *shoulds* in my life. I should write. I love the sense of accomplishment when I write. The accomplishment feeds my ego which is in little need of nourishment. But the *shoulds* cause anxiety and pressure.

Holy Spirit, come sit with me as I write. Breathe into me divine purpose.

Jesus, older brother, let Your obedience to the mission of God in this world shape my thinking, compel my actions into submission to the Father's purposes for me.

Father, God of all of time and eternity, grant me a sense of Your presence that takes me into the place of eternity where my puny world is absorbed into all Your treasures of wisdom and knowledge so that my writing credibly reflects Your heart.

Johnese Burtram

Writing your own prayers for yourself as a writer

May God show you how to pray for yourself so you can plug into His strength. May He make you into His writer — the writer you are meant to be.

What is your biggest personal challenge as a writer? (Despair? Unfulfilled dreams? Problem relationships? Balance in your life?)

How do you want God to support you and touch you as a writer?

Write prayers for yourself as a writer

Prayers for Your Writing

Excellence in Writing

Excellence in writing is about honing and practicing the craft of writing so that it communicates well and conforms to the highest standards in the field of writing. Writing with excellence is your act of worship to God. You want your writing to be of the very best quality — not just to reach the most people with the greatest beauty and be respected in the reading world, but also because you represent the greatest God, worthy of your best work.

Lord, give me time to read, read, read. I give You thanks for books and all written communication. What an amazing way You have given me to improve my writing — I learn to write by reading. Such joy there is to find a book or an article that can be a lifelong friend, a traveling companion. They become part of me.

Father, when I find an article or book that is well-written, let me study how the writing is done. Then give me time to practice writing, to reread what I have written, and rewrite, strengthening any weak places. I long to learn to write by writing.

Father, teach me to plan deliberately as a prelude to my writing, and then I will be prepared to revise the plan as my thoughts develop during the writing process.

Lord God, sharpen my observation skills so that I can put detail and variety into my writing. Lord, You know this is important for all writing, but it is the lifeblood of fiction. Expand my command of nouns and verbs, and help me use adjectives and adverbs judiciously, so that my writing has "toughness and color." I covet Your help.

Father, in writing fiction, help me use all six senses. Don't let the details that come from using the senses atrophy in my writing, as if the characters or readers have lost part of their humanity. Give me a way to communicate the sixth sense, the imaginative aspect in the context of the story that people sense is there, but do not see.

Lord, let me learn and stick to the laws of composition — using positive statements, using parallel construction, using the active voice. Please remind me regularly of the principles of good usage and form so that I may communicate my message well.

Lord, You know where my writing is weak and why. Please teach me to self-edit, fearlessly cutting even my pet phrases when necessary for the larger mission of the piece I'm working on.

Father, grace me with writers who will accompany me on the writing journey. I need good readers and expert editors so I can make my writing the best it can possibly be. With their help, my work can be polished to a shine.

Lord God, I need Your help to craft the crucible my characters must go through. Make my story a record of how my main character fights death — physical, psychological, or spiritual. Help me make the stakes high.

Father, I know I need to avoid unexpected saviors or improbable events to bring my story to a conclusion. Help me keep the unwritten contract with the reader who expects the main character to overcome by strength of character. Show me how to set in place the circumstance and rationale for an intervention earlier in the book.

Father, I covet a daily obedience to writing. Help me write every day; don't let me give in to writer's block.

Dear God,

I am such a perfectionist. Even though I know only You are without fault, I still strive for perfection. When I fail, as expected, I get so down on myself and want to just forget this writing gig. The specter of failure keeps me bound in fear. I think, "If failure is all I can expect, why should I try."

Lord, please help me to trust in Your call to me to write and in Your ability to rewrite my failures into messages that bring You honor and hope to my readers.
With You, God of all grace, I exchange ashes for beauty and my heavy spirit for a garment of praise.

Johnese Burtram

Father God,

Praise You for who You are: Creator, Healer, Redeemer, Reconciler, and Friend. Thank You for the gift of Your written Word that has endured the ages, and for writers today who continue to proclaim Your message of love and truth.

As we wait in Your presence, fill us with the knowledge of who You are and how we fit into Your divine plan. May we see what You see, hear what You hear, and write what is on Your heart.

Keep our eyes focused on You and our hearts pure so that we will only convey words inspired by Your Holy Spirit. May we be diligent in our pursuit of excellence as we learn the writing craft, persevere in editing, and publish documents that bring You honor and glory.

Guide us in using social media and other resources wisely. When we struggle, give us humble, teachable spirits to receive instruction from experienced writers within the writing community. May we unselfishly encourage and strengthen others.

Forgive us for thinking we can do anything without You. Deliver us from the fear of man, fear of failure, and fear of the unknown paths where You might lead. Take away our prideful, stubborn hearts and replace them with hearts of love submitted to You.

We pray Your anointing upon each book, each article, each blog, and each post, and upon the readers within our spheres of influence. May they receive Your message of hope with joy and thanksgiving. Surround each reader with the presence and power of Your Holy Spirit to heal, cleanse, and restore them to the fellowship of Your dear Son, Jesus. In His name we offer this prayer. Amen.

Claudette Renalds

Father, let my writing stay grounded in the real world, full of the detail of life: "[T]he miracle of a maple tree bark, …the cracks in a sidewalk, …the smell of salty pretzels, the beat of the sun at the high altitudes, the lonely cry of a train whistle across cornfields, the slight twist in the dying man's nose, the gait of the border collie, the pulled-back hair of the high school volleyball player, the bleary-eyed determination of this one girl with a head cold, trudging to school among all the other students." [24]

Betsey Kodat

The Sovereign LORD has given me a well-instructed tongue, to know the word that sustains the weary.
Isaiah 50:4a (NIV)

Dear God, Holy Trinity,

You who are the ultimate Author of both the greatest Book ever written and the Author of our very lives, we ask You to guide us into this writing craft that You have called each one of us to undertake.

Help us commit our time to Your will and ordering. Help us to diligently set aside focused time to allow You to speak to our hearts the words You want us to say. Let the words that bring You honor and glory be the only words that flow through our minds, our mouths, and our hands as we bring them into physical form on paper.

What You have spoken to our spirits let flow through us to the benefit of all who would pick up our books and take the time to read them. Help us, Lord, to always be sensitive to Your voice at the very moment You choose to speak regardless of what we are doing or the schedule we feel we need to keep.

As Your servant the prophet Samuel said, *Speak Lord, for your servant is listening,* (1 Samuel 3:9, NASB) so we also echo his words, "Speak Lord, Your servants are listening." What do You want each of us to say to our generation and the spheres of influence You have graciously placed us in?

We are ever grateful for the opportunity to write, to teach, and to continue to grow. Use us for the sake of Your great Name, for the sake of the lost and hurting, and for the encouragement of Your weary Church.

In Jesus' holy, precious name we pray, Amen.

Sahar Smith

Holy Father, Holy Son, Holy Spirit

Holy Father, May Your creative excellence shine through this jar of clay.

I humble myself before You as I write today, being mindful of the fact that I am but dust — a speck that is here today and gone tomorrow.

Holy Son, You are the Living Word and the Light of the world.

May I not stray from the path of righteousness as I communicate my ideas and reveal my heart.
May my writing bring You glory and honor and praise.

Holy Spirit, turn my thoughts away from earthly things and onto eternal truths.

I stake my writing on the truth of scripture, a sure foundation to guard against the attacks of the enemy.

Amen and Amen.

Stephanie Buckwalter

Let the favor of the Lord our God be upon us, and establish the work of our hands upon us; yes, establish the work of our hands!
Psalm 90:17 (ESV)

Writing your own prayers for excellent writing

May God continually help you to improve your craft to His glory and for your joy. May He make you into a writer of excellence. May He teach you to carry out your task prayerfully.

What do you need to do to improve your writing? (Ask someone for help? Read a book? Find a critique group? Write daily?)

What is your biggest difficulty in writing right now? (Dialogue? Making logical connections? Developing your voice? Being brief?)

Write your prayers for excellence in writing

Common Writing Issues

Writing is a very individual activity. Everyone has skills and disabilities, strengths and personality quirks — as individual as our accents or our life experiences. But no matter how seasoned a writer, you need God's astounding power to communicate. You need His facility with new ideas, His wisdom to circumnavigate your writing problems. And He has invited you to ask Him for what you need.

If you're running a 26-mile marathon, remember that every mile is run one step at a time. If you are writing a book, do it one page at a time. If you're trying to master a new language, try it one word at a time. There are 365 days in the average year. Divide any project by 365 and you'll find that no job is all that intimidating.[25]

Chuck Swindoll

Father, help me hone my message — refine it even as I write. Send me a dream, a vision, a joy to work towards. Without the vitality of Your inspiration, my writing will be as lifeless as the dessert without rain, as dark and impenetrable as night in the Antarctic, as deflated as a child whose dream is always out of reach. Support my writing with hope and truth and beauty.

Father, my times are in Your hands (Psalm 31:15). Be with me as I write. Guide my writing process. Tell me what to skip and what to concentrate on. May the world benefit from the way You orchestrate my work.

Father, writing is a solitary endeavor; it takes focused, undivided time to do it well. I ask You to keep me company and secure the boundaries of these moments so that I may produce good writing to Your glory.

Father, let my words nestle down into the hearts of those who read my words.

Almighty God, I need a mentor, someone to come alongside me who knows the craft of writing and knows me. I look to You to help me find that person.

Father, let me support other writers, not for my own reputation, or to use them, but because You work through us all. Your glory always includes good for other people.

Lord, when my work is ready, help me get the message out. Show me the right editor, the right publisher, the readers who are waiting for what I have to say. Make me fearless and trusting that You will use my work for the purpose You have designed for it.

Father,

I have this task: To create in writing a representation of Your world, to make characters that seem to be real folks, who live and love and have their being in a real setting, who respond to their environment in real ways. Help me do my research and then be inspired to write so that the true complexity and interrelatedness of the world makes a strong sturdy foundation to support my writing.

Help me to know Your world and so my writing may mirror it. Let me be with what is physical. ...May my characters, my themes, my images, my settings, my plots, my metaphors, my language, my tones — come out of the world — the "extraordinary, mundane, knowable, confusing, healing, broken, moving, exasperating world that we find around us."[26]

Betsey Kodat

Let Thy Spirit be in our minds, to guide our thoughts
     towards the truth.
Let Thy Spirit be in our hearts, to cleanse them from every
     evil and unclean desire.
Let Thy Spirit be upon our lips, to preserve us from all
     wrong speaking, and to help us by our words to
     commend Thee unto others.
Let Thy Spirit be upon our eyes, that they may find no
     delight in looking on forbidden things, but that they
     may be fixed on Jesus.
Let Thy Spirit be upon our hands that they may be faithful
     in work and eager in service.[27]

William Barclay

Writing your own prayers for your writing issues

Make note of writing issues you want to improve so you can ask for God's help. You can also ask God to help you know what you need so you can ask for His help. May He give you perseverance and joy in the task of improving yourself.

It takes self-awareness to know how to improve yourself as a writer. What do you believe is your biggest struggle or stumbling block with writing? (Lack of inspiration, time constraints, research, starting, procrastination, finding a critique group, editor, publisher, marketing, writers' block, unfulfilled ambition, rejection, managing success?)

Write prayers for your writing issues

Whisper Prayers

Whisper prayers are short prayers that can be prayed in rhythm with breathing; they focus on an immediate sense of need. Developed to be said whenever you sense the need for God's presence, these short prayers serve to draw your focus back to God in an instant. Whisper prayers are easy to memorize. You can pray these one-sentence prayers throughout your day. They make it possible to pray continually, as the Apostle Paul urges. (1 Thessalonians 5:17)

Father, be my strength today.

God, be the heart of everything I do today.

All to Jesus, I surrender.

Be still and know that I am God.

Holy Spirit, You are welcome here.

Lord, may I sow truth to reap righteousness.

God of all truth, plant truth in my writing to combat the lies.

Lord Jesus Christ, have mercy on me, a sinner. (The Jesus Prayer)

May my writing call to souls thirsty for Your truth.

Fill me with Your presence, Lord.

You are my shelter.

Walk beside me through this writing journey, Lord.

How lovely are the feet of Him who brings good news.

Lord, set my feet on high places.

Lord, lift me up on eagle's wings.

Write Your Word on the tablet of my heart.

Come, Lord Jesus, help me.

Jesus, help me not to give up or give in!

Lord, help me through another day.

O Lord, please help me begin again.

God, help me fight to the end and finish the course.

God, be the heart of everything I do today.

You are my hiding place.

Lord, free me from care for myself.

God, I invite You into my life.

Lord, You are my hope.

Jesus, be my light.

Lord, be with me.

Have Your way, God.

Yes, Lord.

Holy Spirit, renew my mind.

God, Your kingdom come, Your will be done in me.

Jesus, You are Lord.

Lord, You are enough.

Submissions from Stephanie Buckwalter,
Johnese Burtram, Betsey Kodat, Ruth West

Whisper Prayers from Scripture

These whisper prayers are paraphrases of Bible verses, adapted to make them personal.

May your Word be a lamp to my feet and a light to my path. (Psalm 119:105)

We look to Jesus, the author and finisher of our faith. (Hebrews 12:2)

God,
You have not given us the spirit of fear, but of power, love, and a sound mind.
(2 Timothy 1:7)

God,
Your Word is quick and more powerful than a double-edged sword, dividing bone and marrow.
(Hebrews 4:12)

Life and death are in the power of the tongue. May we speak and write words that bring life.
(Proverbs 18:21)

God,
May we honor You in our obedience and faith, may our words and works honor You!
(James 2)

Because of the service by which you have proved yourselves, others will praise God for the obedience that accompanies your confession of the gospel of Christ, and for your generosity in sharing with them and with everyone else.
(2 Corinthians 9:13)

This is the covenant I will make with them after that time, says the Lord. I will put my laws in their hearts, and I will write them on their minds.
(Hebrews 10:16)

May He give you the desire of your heart and make all your plans succeed. May we shout for joy over your victory and lift up our banners in the name of our God. May the Lord grant all your requests.
(Psalm 20:4-5)

Whisper prayers from scripture submitted by Sharon Holmes

Writing your own whisper prayers

May God give you a sentence or a phrase that you can pray throughout the day to welcome Him into your writing.

Craft a short — even one sentence — prayer that you can use to weave God into your day as you write.

Write your whisper prayers

Scripture Prayers

We need to harness the synergy of the Holy Spirit in our personal writing. He who inspired the writers of the Bible can make sure your writing serves God's purposes. The best way of having this happen is to pray from the scripture itself. Scripture grounds our work in God. Praying scripture empowers us. It empowers our prayer. It empowers our writing.

In the morning, Lord, You hear my voice; in the morning, I lay my request before You and wait expectantly for what You will do for me as I write. Father, help me guard my heart, for everything I write flows from it. Keep my words free of perversity; keep me from corrupt talk. Let my eyes look straight ahead, focusing on whatever is true, noble, and right, whatever is pure, lovely, and admirable. If anything is excellent or praiseworthy — let me write and think such things. May I take careful thought to the plots or characters or logical arguments I create. May all my writing be steadfast in all Your ways. Above all, let all my words tell the truth in love. Fill my writing with love, joy, peace, patience, kindness, goodness, faithfulness, gentleness, and self-control.
(Psalm 5:1-3, Proverb 4:23-26, Philippians 4:8, Ephesians 4:18, Galatians 5:22-23, all NIV)

Betsey Kodat

Psalm 23 for Writers

The Lord is the Author and Perfecter of my faith, I will trust
and obey.
   His Word guides my thoughts and ideas —
      therefore, His Truth shines through what I write.
   He strengthens my faith.
   He leads me to live out the gospel for His name's sake.

Even though I walk through the valley of this worldly
system that is antagonistic toward all that is of God,
   I will fear no evil for You are with me.
   Your correction and Your guidance comfort me.

You prepare my place on the internet in the presence of
   my enemies.
You anoint my writing with power, my writing reflects
   Your character.

Surely goodness and mercy shall follow me
   as my words are published for all to see.
I will rest in the shadow of the Almighty for protection.
I will stand firm on His promises,
   triumphing over evil by the blood of the Lamb
   and the word of my testimony.
And when all is said and done,
I will dwell in the house of the Lord forever.

Stephanie Buckwalter

Dear Lord,

I need to ask for Your help. I sometimes feel weak and tired, like my creativity is strained and empty. I sometimes feel like my writing is hollow and uninspiring.

I feel discouraged and criticize and devalue myself. I feel like others are succeeding while I am not. I feel insecure and filled with worry and anxiety, wondering if anyone will be blessed by my writing. Will anyone buy it and like it? Will they tell others about it? I am afraid my marketing will fall flat. I think that my writing will be lost in the vast cacophony of what is already out there.

But then I force myself to remember You. I remember that You have promised, *My grace is sufficient for you, for my power is made perfect in weakness.* (2 Corinthians 12:9, NIV) Like Paul, I will boast all the more gladly about my weaknesses, so that Christ's power may rest on me. I trust and believe that I am receiving Your power, Your strength, Your endurance.

I remember You are the one *who comforts us in all our troubles.* (2 Corinthians 1:4, NIV) You ease my worries. You cheer me, encourage me, and lift me up. You say, *Those who hope in the LORD will renew their strength. They will soar on wings like eagles; they will run and not grow weary, they will walk and not be faint.* (Isaiah 40:31, NIV) Thank You, thank You!

When I feel dry and parched and uncreative, I remember that You tell us You are *making a way in the wilderness and streams in the wasteland.* (Isaiah 43:19, NIV)

When I feel like I lack wisdom and knowledge that I need in my writing, I remind myself that You tell me, *If any of you lacks wisdom, let him ask God, who gives generously to all without reproach, and it will be given him.* (James 1:5, ESV) and, *An intelligent heart acquires knowledge, and the ear of the wise seeks knowledge.* (Proverbs 18:15, ESV)

When I feel torn down, I remember *I can do all things through Him who strengthens me.* (Philippians 4:13, ESV) *And we know that for those who love God all things work together for good, for those who are called according to His purpose.* (Romans 8:28, ESV)

In all this I feel encouraged. I boldly proclaim, *thanks be to God, who always leads us as captives in Christ's triumphal procession and uses us to spread the aroma of the knowledge of him everywhere.* (2 Corinthians 2:14, NIV)

We are triumphant in him!

Joe Gelak

Let the words of my mouth and the meditations of my heart be acceptable in thy sight, O Lord, my strength and my redeemer.
Psalm 19:14 (KJV)

20 Scriptures to Pray for Your Writing

1. Pray that you would write not in your own power but equipped with God's power. *But you will receive power when the Holy Spirit comes on you; and you will be my witnesses in Jerusalem, and in all Judea and Samaria, and to the ends of the earth.* (Acts 1:8, NIV)

2. Pray that you would be focused on your calling and purpose as a writer. *The Spirit of the Lord is on me, because he has anointed me to proclaim good news to the poor. He has sent me to proclaim freedom for the prisoners and recovery of sight for the blind, to set the oppressed free, to proclaim the year of the Lord's favor.* (Luke 4:18-19, NIV)

3. Pray that you would be focused on God's approval, more than approval from others. *For am I now seeking the approval of man, or of God? Or am I trying to please man? If I were still trying to please man, I would not be a servant of Christ.* (Galatians 1:10, ESV)

4. Pray against Satan's attacks regarding your worth as a writer/blogger. *Put on the full armor of God…so that when the day of evil comes, you may be able to stand your ground, and after you have done everything, to stand.* (Ephesians 6:11, 13, NIV)

5. Pray that you would share God's messages without fear. *Pray also for me, that whenever I speak, words may be given me so that I will fearlessly make known the mystery of the gospel, for which I am an ambassador in chains. Pray that I may declare it fearlessly, as I should.* (Ephesians 6:19-20, NIV)

6. Pray that you would be obedient to your calling to write. *I will come and proclaim your mighty acts, Sovereign LORD; I will proclaim your righteous deeds, yours alone. Since my youth, God, you have taught me, and to this day I declare your marvelous deeds. Even when I am old and gray, do not forsake me, my God, till I declare your power to the next generation, your mighty acts to all who are to come.* (Psalm 71:16-18, NIV)

7. Pray for wisdom regarding your writing ministry. *If any of you lacks wisdom, you should ask God, who gives generously to all without finding fault, and it will be given to you.* (James 1:5, NIV)

8. Pray that you would be diligent to continue sharing God's message with others through your writing and in every aspect of your life. *Until I come, devote yourself to the public reading of Scripture, to preaching and to teaching. Do not neglect your gift, which was given you through prophecy when the body of elders laid their hands on you. Be diligent in these matters; give yourself wholly to them, so that everyone may see your progress.* (1 Timothy 4:13-15, NIV)

9. Pray that you would find a godly writing community, or if you're already part of one, that you would be an encouraging member. *And let us consider how we may spur one another on toward love and good deeds, not giving up meeting together, as some are in the habit of doing, but encouraging one another--and all the more as you see the Day approaching.* (Hebrews 10:24-25, NIV)

10. Pray that those who need to read your message will find it and be changed by it. *For this reason, since the day we heard about you, we have not stopped praying for*

you. We continually ask God to fill you with the knowledge of his will through all the wisdom and understanding that the Spirit gives. (Colossians 1:9, NIV)

11. Pray that you would not get distracted by comparing your writing ministry and your platform to others'. *[W]e will not compare ourselves with each other as if one of us were better and another worse. We have far more interesting things to do with our lives. Each of us is an original.* (Galatians 5:26, MSG)

12. Pray that you would not get discouraged from writing. *Therefore, since through God's mercy we have this ministry, we do not lose heart.* (2 Corinthians 4:1, NIV)

13. Pray that you would use the word of God accurately to encourage and teach others. *All Scripture is God-breathed and is useful for teaching, rebuking, correcting and training in righteousness, so that the servant of God may be thoroughly equipped for every good work.* (2 Timothy 3:16-17, NIV)

14. Pray that your writing ministry would be blessed. *...'Oh, that you would bless me and enlarge my territory! Let your hand be with me'...* (1 Chronicles 4:10, NIV)

15. Pray that your words will have the power to nurture and heal. *Pleasant words are a honeycomb, Sweet to the soul and healing to the bones.* (Proverbs 16:24, NASB)

16. Pray that you would be patient with where God has you in your writing journey. *The seed that fell among thorns stands for those who hear, but as they go on their way they are choked by life's worries, riches and pleasures and they do not mature. But the seed on good soil stands*

for those with a noble and good heart, who hear the word, retain it, and by persevering produce a crop. (Luke 8:14-15, NIV)

17. Pray that God would use your stories to impact His kingdom in your writing ministry. *And they overcame him [Satan] by the blood of the Lamb and by the word of their testimony.* (Revelation 12:11a, NASB)

18. Pray that you would persevere in your writing efforts, despite obstacles or discouragement. *And let us not grow weary of doing good, for in due season we will reap, if we do not give up.* (Galatians 6:9, ESV)

19. Pray that you and your writing would be completely surrendered to God and used for His glory. *Therefore, I urge you, brothers and sisters, in view of God's mercy, to offer your bodies as a living sacrifice, holy and pleasing to God--this is your true and proper worship.* (Romans 12:1, NIV)

20. Pray that God would equip you with all you need to accomplish His will in your writing ministry. *Now may the God of peace...equip you with everything good for doing his will, and may he work in us what is pleasing to him, through Jesus Christ, to whom be glory for ever and ever. Amen.* (Hebrews 13:20-21, NIV)

Jenn Seohnlin

Jesus, you are the Word. Your Word created all that exists. Your Word speaks life into our dead spirits. Your Word calls forth fruitfulness in all who are called by Your name.

I thank You for the words Your Holy Spirit calls out of us. Let us write Your words in our own voice, reflective of Your work in our lives. Let the words we write affirm Your nature and call into life those who read our writing. As Your Word is effective to Your intended purpose, let our words be used to Your intentions as well.

Johnese Burtram

Writing your own scripture prayers

May God's word be the foundation of your writing life. May He give you His words to undergird your words and make them shine in the world and achieve His highest purpose.

Have you run across a verse recently which you want to pray for your writing? Choose a relevant scripture and turn it into a prayer, like this:

May the grace of the Lord Jesus Christ, and the love of God, and the fellowship of the Holy Spirit be with all of you.
(2 Corinthians 13:14, NIV)

Prayer: Lord Jesus, send your grace; Father, send your love; Holy Spirit, send your fellowship into my writing. I need them now.

Write your scripture prayers

Personalized Prayer

"Prewritten prayers (often referred to as liturgical prayer) are a wonderful resource for the spiritual life. Scripture recast as prayer provides consistent and thoughtful content. Regular use of a liturgy enables us to pray with clarity and in alignment with biblical truth regardless of how we are feeling on a particular day." We can find relevant scripture to apply to our writing, and can help you "stay centered in Jesus and reliant on Him."[28]

Example
Father, I present myself to You, the One who knows me inside out. I need You to be with me as I write. You are the Master writer who knows everything from start to finish. You know what my readers need — what Your world needs — and what my role in it is. Please strengthen my writing today. I need You in this process — I give this time to You to inspire and guide me.

When we rely upon organization, we get what organization can do; when we rely upon education, we get what education can do; when we rely upon eloquence, we get what eloquence can do. And so on. But when we rely upon prayer, we get what God can do.[29]

A.C. Dixon

Writing your own personalized prayer

May God bless you with words to say before you begin your writing, words which ground you in His life, words which free you to trust God's work in you.

What do I need to remember every time I sit down to write? To sense God's presence with me? For fresh inspiration? For perseverance? To leave my worries behind? Not to be side-tracked from the purpose for my work?

Write your personalized prayer

Submitting Your Work to God

There comes a time when you have to finish your work. Sometimes writers do this easily — often with a sigh of relief — but then we feel like there is so much more we can or should do. Sol Stein said that authors are never finished writing until their book is published. Submitting your work to God is basically handing it over to Him and letting it go. That is the best place for it, after all. Whatever influence our work ultimately has is up to God.

Dear Lord,

We want our writing and our words to be Your thoughts and ideas and feelings flowing through us. We want to be Your reflection and instrument and vessel and channel and portal to those around us with all we write. You call us to be a *letter from Christ...written not with ink but with the Spirit of the living God, not on tablets of stone but on tablets of human hearts.* (2 Corinthians 3:3, NIV)

Please help us to submit and surrender and give ourselves to You completely and entirely, as Your followers and servants and writers. We do not want to just write for our own satisfaction or pleasure, or to impress others, or to make money, or to build a reputation. We want our primary desire to be pleasing You. To build Your kingdom. To be used by You to bless and help others.

You are the Designer and Creator of all. You are the Master Artist, the great Writer of Life. Even our bodies are written by You through DNA and our genes. We remember that our writing capability is exclusively from You, a gift. Thank You for this gift. We want to use it as the servant with the five talents that put the money entrusted to him to work and earned a good return for his master, as told by Jesus in Matthew 25:14-30. We want to be fruitful for You, oh God. We hope and pray that all we write will reflect Your heart and mind. Messages of hope and love and joy and peace and faith.

We pray in the name of Jesus, Amen.

Joe Gelak

Unless the LORD builds the house, the
builders labor in vain.
Unless the LORD watches over the city,
the guards stand watch in vain.
Psalm 127:1 (NIV)

This favorite hymn is a song of total submission. Apply its stanzas as preparation for writing.

Take My Life and Let It Be

Take my life, and let it be
Consecrated, Lord, to Thee;
Take my moments and my days,
Let them flow in ceaseless praise,
Let them flow in ceaseless praise.

Take my hands, and let them move
At the impulse of Thy love;
Take my feet and let them be
Swift and beautiful for Thee,
Swift and beautiful for Thee.

Take my voice, and let me sing
Always, only, for my King;
Take my lips, and let them be
Filled with messages from Thee,
Filled with messages from Thee.

Take my silver and my gold;
Not a mite would I withhold;
Take my intellect, and use
Every power as Thou shalt choose,
Every power as Thou shalt choose.

Take my will and make it Thine;
It shall be no longer mine.
Take my heart; it is Thine own;
It shall be Thy royal throne,
It shall be Thy royal throne.

Take my love; my Lord, I pour
At Thy feet its treasure-store.
Take myself, and I will be
Ever, only, all for Thee,
Ever, only, all for Thee.

Frances Ridley Havergal, 1774

Father,

I trust in You.
I commit everything I write to Your purpose.

As I write, send me Your inspiration,
Your direction, and Your beauty of expression.

I may become engrossed in my work and forget this
prayer —
but I trust You to be present in every session of writing.
In Jesus' name, Amen.

Betsey Kodat

O Infinite Creator…
Do Thou, who givest speech to the tongue of little children,
instruct my tongue
and pour into my lips the grace of Thy benediction.
Give me keenness of apprehension,
capacity of remembering, method
and ease in learning, insight in interpretation,
and copious eloquence in speech.
Instruct my beginning, direct my progress,
and set Thy seal upon the finished work,
Thou, who are true God and true Man,
who livest and reignest, world without end.[30]

Thomas Aquinas

Lord,

I devote this writing time to You. I ask for the blessing of Moses on Levi, son of Jacob, *"Bless all [my] skills, LORD, and be pleased with the work of [my] hands."* (Deuteronomy 33:11, NIV) Let this devoted time be pleasing to You. Inspiring words, clarity of communication, artistry of phrase come from You.

I dedicate myself to listen carefully to Your still small voice and write as You direct. Keep me from grievous error.

Let these words find favor with those who read them. May Your gracious Spirit draw the readers to the message You have for them. Let Your Spirit speak louder than anything I would say on my own.

As I am obedient to Your call and apply myself with diligence to the task, the results are up to You.

In as much as I have spoken Your word as Your spokesperson, let it go forth in power and authority to accomplish that purpose for which You sent it.

This I commit to You.

Johnese Burtram

Father God,

I devote my writing to You. I declare that I rely on You for everything. I want to write today in the counsel and power of the Holy Spirit, in company with Jesus.

I place my life and work in Your hands. I praise and thank You for everything that will happen in my life and work — the planned and unplanned, the serendipity and the expected. At the end of the day, remind me to sit and take note of what You have done and to thank You.

Betsey Kodat

"Dear Lord, the pages are finished. At least, I think they're finished. And now it's time to send them out into the world — my words into your world. Let me, Lord, release them, and let me, oh let me not want anything out of them but what good You will do with them. ...Lord, let the words serve. ...[L]et them speak well to those whom you mean to hear. Then, Lord, I will know that what you gave me to work with, I have worked with; and what You gave me to use, I have used. Everything after that is up to You; so let me leave it in your hands. And Lord, one thing more: Tomorrow, of your goodness, give me another blank page, and in your mercy, set me to it."[31]

Gary Schmidt

> *Therefore, do not be anxious about tomorrow, for tomorrow will be anxious for itself. Sufficient for the day is its own trouble.*
> Matthew 6:34 (ESV)

Dear Jesus,

I pray for contentment along my writing journey. Capture my anxious thoughts, my uncertainties, my wrongful desires. Help me to rest in the knowledge that You have called me to write. Let me not be distracted by lack of success. Let me not be discouraged by setbacks. Let me not be depressed by writer's block.

Instead, let me rejoice in my calling. Let me seek to glorify You first, men second. Let my focus be on writing the stories, poems, prayers, articles, and books You have put on my heart. Let my desire be to please You and You alone with the words I put down on paper.

Give me a contented heart with where I am along my writing journey. Help me to see Your hand in my writing, and to be satisfied with my place in the writing world. Help me to seek excellence, not for my own pride, but because it brings glory to You.

When discontentment raises its ugly head, let me recognize its many disguises. Give me the strength to yank it out of my writing and thoughts as one weeds a garden. Help me to live a writing life of contentment, rejoicing always in where You have placed me and in the words You have given me.

Oh, Lord, let me not grow weary along this journey. Give me patience and perseverance. May Your face shine upon me as I write, and may I embody contentment even in the face of difficulties, setbacks, and challenges. Amen.

Sarah Hamaker

"All to Jesus I surrender..."

I have sung these words since I was a tiny girl. But it's so hard, Lord.

I have really enjoyed writing; this sweet spot of mine holding so much pleasure, satisfaction, and that prized sense of accomplishment. I have worked hard and I feel good.

But, O Jesus, You know the critique can feel so brutal, even if unintended. So I must strive to write beyond censure. I will revise...and revise...and revise. When I finally cease the circular pattern of changes, I weep in frustrated exhaustion at my inability to capture this elusive perfection.

So, this I decide, Lord; "I surrender all...All to Thee, my blessed Savior..." I relinquish my control on this project to You. You *always* take care of what is Yours. You will take care of me and my writing. You will cause Your work in me to flourish and accomplish Your will.

I will trust in You.

Johnese Burtram

All to Jesus I Surrender

All to Jesus I surrender,
All to Him I freely give;
I will ever love and trust Him,
In His presence daily live.

All to Jesus I surrender,
Humbly at His feet I bow, …
Take me, Jesus, take me now.

All to Jesus I surrender,
Make me, Savior, wholly Thine; …
Truly know that Thou art mine.

All to Jesus I surrender,
Lord, I give myself to Thee; …
Let Thy blessing fall on me.

All to Jesus I surrender,
Now I feel the sacred flame.
Oh, the joy of full salvation!
Glory, glory to His name!

Judson W. Van DeVenter, 1869

Father,

Help me to bundle up my crowded thoughts and leave them with You. You are able to do what I cannot. I know You can make them a bundle of beauty, though I cannot imagine how.

I confess that I love this piece of work. I have spent so much time with it; it is like a child to me, a part of myself. And I need to let it go and let You take it from here. I release this work to the future and purpose You have for it.

Father, it is time to disengage from my hard work, and let it be done. I leave my writing in Your capable hands.

Betsey Kodat

Commit your way to the LORD;
trust in Him, and He will do it.
He will bring forth your righteousness like
the dawn,
your justice like the noonday sun.
Psalm 37:5-6 (NIV)

Lord,

Without You I can do nothing of eternal value. Take my words, my thoughts, my ideas and give them Your power to make a difference in the world and for eternity.

Stephanie Buckwalter

Trust in the LORD with all your heart,
and lean not on your own understanding;
in all your ways acknowledge Him,
and He will make your paths straight.
Proverbs 3:5-6 (NIV)

Writing your own prayers for submitting your work to God

When your piece of writing is finished, it is time to give it to God as an offering. Praise God for what makes it easy to let your finished work go and praise God for what makes it hard to let it go. Praise God that He will carry it forward to the purpose which He has for it.

May God help you know when your work is complete. When this moment comes, may He help you feel a sense of accomplishment. May you lift up your work to God, as a sweet offering.

Write your prayers for submitting your work to God

Blessings for Writers

Blessing others is an incredible privilege — to bless is to declare that God's favor will rest on others. It is a form of prayer that expresses the highest confidence that God will deliver the good we declare for the people we are blessing. Actively blessing other writers expands the kingdom of God through writing and also stretches your heart to love and include others in the fellowship of writing.

A Writer's Blessing

May you use the time you have to write, writing.
May the words flow freely from your mind to your fingers.
May you create truth in the stories you tell.
May you bring Christ to your readers, even if you never mention His name.
May you see success in your writing, however God chooses to bring that about.
May you be content where God has placed you along your writing journey.
May you give encouragement to other writers.
May you find joy in your writing.

Sarah Hamaker

> *"The Spirit of the Lord is on me,*
> *because he has anointed me*
> *to proclaim good news to the poor.*
> *He has sent me to proclaim freedom for*
> *the prisoners*
> *and recovery of sight for the blind,*
> *to set the oppressed free,*
> *to proclaim the year of the Lord's favor."*
> Luke 4:18-20 (NIV)

Almighty God,

Bless my fellow writers with powerful words which can do good for the world.

Bless my fellow writers with joy in their writing. May they see the fruit of their labor.

Bless my fellow writers with hope and vision.

Shower Your goodness on my fellow writers who write words or songs, who craft blogs or emails or movies or tweets or visual display or Instagram. Give them the thrill of seeing their vision become a reality and serve Your dreams for Your world.

Betsey Kodat

Heavenly Father,

Bless me with confidence in the anointing You have given me to write. *Behold, I am the servant of the Lord; let it be to me according to your word.* (Luke 1:38, ESV)

Open my eyes and ears and heart to hear Your whispers of truth and love You have for me and those You want me to share them with.

Protect me from the lies and deceit of the evil one. May I rest confidently in Your truths and in my anointing, rather than getting sidetracked by doubts, insecurities, and distractions.

Bless my writing ministry, Father God. May my pen flow with Your words and the message burning in my heart to share with others, to bring healing and hope to hurting hearts.

Open doors so that I can get my words in front of readers who need these truths.

Bless my writing time, that it would be productive and fruitful.

May I be able to grasp how and wide and deep and long is Your love for me as I write and always. Amen.

Jenn Soehnlin

A Blessing for Writers

Bless my hands that I may work diligently in my writing.

Bless my heart that is filled with Your love
    so that it comes out in my writing.

Bless my mind that I may take captive every thought,
    sentence, paragraph, and line of verse
    so that I may submit it to Your will.

Bless my stories that they may reflect His story.

Bless my words that they may be pleasing in Your sight.

Bless my relationships that I may
    reflect Your love to my readers always.

Bless how I view my work that I may remain humble
    and write for an audience of One
    —though hundreds or even thousands praise my work.

Stephanie Buckwalter

I have work to do, I have a busy world around me; eye, ear,
and thought will all be needed for that work, done in and
amidst that busy world; now, ere I enter upon it, I would
commit eye, ear, thought, and wish to thee. Do thou bless
them and keep their work thine…[32]

Thomas Arnold

Praying for our Readers

Lord God, I write so that others may connect to and engage my thoughts and be influenced or entertained or challenged or enlightened by them.

May Your grace enfold us both in the rich fellowship of Your life. In Jesus' name, Amen.

Betsey Kodat

Writer's Blessing

The LORD bless you and keep you as you explore new areas and genres to write in excellence;

The LORD make His face shine on you and be gracious to you as you triumph and experience success in finishing, marketing, and publishing the work God has given you to bless others;

The LORD turn His face toward you and give you peace for the journey into all that He has called you to write. (Numbers 6:24-26)

May He give you the desire of your heart and make all your plans succeed.
May we shout for joy over your victory and lift up our banners in the name of our God.
May the Lord grant all your requests. (Psalm 20:4-5)
Amen.

Sharon Holmes

Blessing on the Writer

God bless you with:
    Clarity of mind
    Discipline to take up the pen
    Humility to listen and seek help where needed
    Courage to write about the hard thing; to write truth
    Generosity of spirit
        To be eager to congratulate your colleagues'
        successes
        To share what you know
        To give your time to those seeking assistance
        To read what others have written
    Wisdom to know what writing projects God has
    assigned to you
    Fortitude to take the steps beyond writing to get your
    God-assigned work available for others.

God bless my writer friends with *power* — the capacity to accomplish God's will (2 Timothy 1:7) — as they give themselves to the awesome endeavor of writing Your message.

Johnese Burtram

Father,

May Your favor rest on my writing friends. Establish their plans and empower their writing as they stay attuned to You.

Holy Spirit, empower their work so that it accomplishes its purpose to glorify You and bless their readers. (Psalm 90:17, NIV; Zechariah 4:6, NIV; Psalm 57:2, KJV)

In Jesus' name, Amen.

Betsey Kodat

Lord,

Bless these writers with a confident sense of Your call to write.
Bless them with pleasure as they follow that call.
Give them joy in the writing.
Give them confidence in the ability You give to accomplish Your will.
Bless them with the favor of agents and publishers.
Let readers find the writers whose message brings light and hope.
Prosper them with fruitfulness.

Johnese Burtram

Writing your own prayers of blessing for writers

May God bless you with words to bless other writers, knowing personally their needs and the power of God to accomplish all things for them.

What do you want for yourself and for other writers?

What can only God give them?

Write your blessings for writers

Answered
Prayers

God's answers to prayer can all-too-easily disappear into the sea of life and be forgotten. To keep this from happening, start a list of all that God has done for you as a writer. Then set aside time to consider your list and ponder what God has done. (Psalm 64:9) Return to this list regularly and add to it as you remember new things. Rereading this list can steady you and embolden both your writing and your praise and thanksgiving.

May God our Father highlight the things He does for you as a writer. Beyond the ordinary avenues of success which speak to you, may He let you see His subtle, almost hidden work. As the evidence of answered prayer mounts up, may your praise also mount up, overflowing into rejoicing and hope.

> *Many, Lord my God, are the wonders you*
> *have done, the things you planned for us.*
> *None can compare with you; were I to*
> *speak and tell of your deeds, they would*
> *be too many to declare.*
> Psalm 40:5 (NIV)

Prayer Requests

Answered Prayers

End Notes

[1] Sally Burke and Cyndie Claypool deNeve, *Raise Them Up*, (Eugene: Harvest House Publishers, 2019), p. 25.

[2] Oswald Chambers in Scott Thompson and Lesley Hackman, *Walking the Path of an Intercessor: Encouragement and Lessons Discovered While Walking the Path of an Intercessor,* (McLean: Self Published, 2013), p. 57.

[3] <https://www.goodreads.com/quotes/12207-you-say-grace-before-meals-all-right-but-i-say> (accessed January 6, 2020)

[4] C. S. Lewis, *Letters to Malcom: Chiefly on Prayer*, (London: Geoffrey Bles, 1964), p. 109.

[5] Martyn Lloyd-Jones Quotes, <http://christian-quotes.ochristian.com/Martyn-Lloyd-Jones-Quotes/page-2.shtml> (accessed January 6, 2020)

[6] Frederick Buechner Quotes, <http://christian-quotes.ochristian.com/Frederick-Buechner-Quotes/page-4.shtml> (accessed January 6, 2020)

[7] Kevin Johnson, Ed. *Pray the Scriptures Bible, God's Word*, (Minneapolis: Bethany House, 2012), p. 43.

[8] Brother Lawrence, <https://gracequotes.org/author-quote/brother-lawrence/> (accessed January 6, 2020)

[9] Gary Schmidt and Elizabeth Stickney, *Acceptable Words*, (Grand Rapids: Eerdmans, 2012), p. 48.

[10] Ibid., pp. 110, 111.

[11] Ibid., p. 110.

[12] *Book of Common Prayer* (N.Y., N.Y.: Church Publishing, Inc., 1986), pp. 836-837.

[13] Schmidt and Stickney, p. 5.

[14] Ibid., p. 85.

[15] Ibid., p. 39.

[16] Ibid., p. 68.

[17] Ibid., pp. 143, 144.

[18] Lindsay Olesberg, *The Bible Study Handbook, A Comprehensive Guide to an Essential Practice* (Downers Grove: Intervarsity Press, 2012), p. 91.

[19] Schmidt and Stickney, p. 125.

[20] Ibid., p. xiv.

[21] Ibid., p. 45.

[22] Ibid., p. 48.

[23] Ibid., p. 81. Prayer based on the writing of Gary Schmidt.

[24] Ibid., pp. 2, 3.

[25] Chuck Swindoll Quotes, <http://christian-quotes.ochristian.com/Chuck-Swindoll-Quotes/page-2.shtml> (accessed January 6, 2020)

[26] Schmidt and Stickney, pp. 2, 3, 18. Prayer based on the writing of Gary Schmidt.

27 Ibid., p. 69.

28 Olesberg, 189.

29 A.C. Dixon Quotes, <http://christian-quotes.ochristian.com/A.C.-Dixon-Quotes/> (accessed January 6, 2020)

30 Schmidt and Stickney, p. 29.

31 Ibid., pp. 158, 159.

32 Ibid., p. 23.

Contributors

Stephanie Buckwalter is an award-winning writer and researcher. She runs a website for parents of children with special needs with a focus on improving their family's quality of life. She loves writing and being out in God's creation. She serves on the board of CCWF in Technical Support. artofspecialneedsparenting.com

Johnese Burtram is the Vice President of CCWF. From 2012 to 2018, she served as Director of Northern Virginia Christian Writers Fellowship. She was contributor, editor, and publisher of NVCWF's annual anthology. She writes to reflect the nature of Jesus and encourage others on their journey of spiritual transformation. She is ordained with the Assemblies of God.

Michele Chynoweth is the best-selling and award-winning author of *The Faithful One, The Peace Maker, The Runaway Prophet* and *The Jealous Son*, contemporary suspense novels that re-imagine Bible stories. She is a sought-after speaker, book coach/editor, college writing instructor, University of Notre Dame grad, and lives in her native Maryland. michelechynoweth.com

Barbara Coulson has been learning from and following Jesus for over half a century. She resides in Northern Virginia with her husband of forty-two years, is the mother of two, mother-in-love of one, grandmother of five, and friend of many. Some of her favorite things are quilting, learning new things, reading, and journaling. Barbara is a blogger and aspiring novelist, and you can read her weekly posts at barbaracoulson.com

Joe Gelak writes about pursuing God through the spiritual journey to become one with Christ. He loves his family, nature, and reading. Psalm 84:5

Sharron Giambanco and her husband own and operate a pizzeria in Northern Virginia. A mom of six children and grandmother to one wonderful granddaughter, Sharron enjoys reading and working on her writing projects, in between waiting on customers, answering phone calls, and the other demands of a small business owner.

Sarah Hamaker is the author of *Hired@Home, Ending Sibling Rivalry, Dangerous Christmas Memories* and *Mistletoe & Murder*. Her stories have appeared in *Chicken Soup for the Soul* books. Sarah is a member of ACFW and ACFW Virginia Chapter, and President of Capital Christian Writers Fellowship. Sarah lives in Virginia with her husband, four children, and three cats. Connect with her at sarahhamakerficiton.com.

Stephen W. Hiemstra (MDiv, PhD) is a slave of Christ, husband of thirty years to Maryam, father of three, author, and volunteer pastor in Hispanic ministry. Stephen writes on Christian spirituality in English and Spanish. He published his most recent book, *Simple Faith*, in April 2019. He blogs four times weekly at T2Pneuma.net, including a podcast on Mondays. t2pneuma.net, stephenwhiemstra.net

Jennifer Hinders is a freelance writer and poet. She has published articles and poems for numerous websites and magazines. Jennifer lives and works out of her home in the Washington, D.C., area, and spends her free time hanging out with her husband and kids. jhinders.com

Sharon Holmes is a licensed minister with the Assemblies of God. She is working towards a Ph.D. in Intercultural Studies. Her primary published works include academic papers. Sharon lives with her husband in Northern Virginia, and they have two married children and two grandchildren.

Betsey Kodat lives with her husband, Roger, in Herndon, Virginia. They have two daughters and a soon-to-be-born granddaughter. Betsey has been writing prayers ever since she married thirty-five years ago. Her life goal is to maximize prayer for her family, friends, church, and world. She has written a book for praying for the persecuted Church, *Arise, Lord!*

Susan A. J. Lyttek, author of five novels, award-winning writer, blogger, wife, and mother to two homeschool graduates, currently escapes her employment search by writing random stories. You can find out more about her and her books at sajlyttek.com.

Claudette Renalds began her writing career at age 67. Several short stories were published in NVCWF anthologies. In February 2019, she published her debut novel, *By the Sea*, a contemporary romance. Her second novel, *Journey to Hope: The Legacy of a Mail Order Bride,* will be released in 2020. thatothersmayknow.blog

Audra Sanlyn is the author of *The Journal* (under the name Audra Johnson) and *Through the Eyes of a Veteran: A History of Winchester,* a memoir/local history based on the life of her husband's grandfather. She stays home with her two children, writes a monthly encouragement blog, and leads her church's youth ministry with her husband. Audrasanlyn.com

Sahar Smith is a lover of the Lord Jesus Christ and a follower of the Holy Spirit. Sahar is a student at Dallas Theological Seminary, Washington, D.C., working on her master's degree in Cross-Cultural Ministries. She joined Heritage Action as a Sentinel to advocate for our biblical and traditional family values in the government sector. Sahar has been married to Alfred for twenty-nine years and has three children and five grandchildren.

Jenn Soehnlin is a middle school English teacher and a mother to two little lads who are precious blessings and who both have special needs. She is the author of *Embracing This Special Life*. Jenn enjoys blogging about faith, praying scripture, and special needs parenting at embracing.life.

Ruth Granados West is a mom of five, married to Bob for twenty-five years. She is an intercessor and enjoys praying with and for others and our nation. She is an auxiliary member of Gideon International and likes to share the gospel through her church's ministries. She is working on a book about her family's immigration to the United States from Mexico. She currently lives in Northern Virginia.

Ann Westerman, retired English and ESOL teacher, has been drawn to writing since she wrote her first poem at age seven. She is an avid journaler, and has written articles and letters to the editor. She writes stories set in Tidewater Virginia, where she grew up. She views the stories — the characters, conflicts, and the choices they make — as an evangelistic tool to share the gospel of Christ and His love for us. anndw22.wordpress.com

David L. Winters is an author and speaker from Kesington, Maryland. After retiring from the Department of Homeland Security in 2015, he began writing full time. His books include *Taking God to Work (The Keys to Ultimate Success)* and *The Accidental Missionary (A Gringo's Love Affair with Peru)*. He also writes for Guideposts, CBN.com, and The Institute for Faith, Work and Economics.

sabbaticalofthemind.net

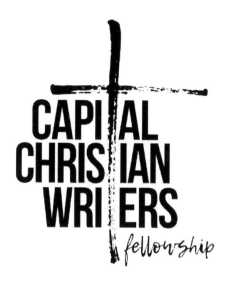

At Capital Christian Writers Fellowship (CCWF), our mission is simple:

To encourage one another in our writing endeavors

and to educate writers, both fiction and nonfiction,

on the craft and business of writing.

The CCWF website is designed to provide resources, information and encouragement for Christian writers and aspiring writers. You can find us at

ccwritersfellowship.org

For bulk orders, please contact us directly through our website.

Made in the USA
Monee, IL
08 February 2020